I0878807

EARTH ON FIRE

EARTH ON FIRE

THE SCIENCE, HISTORY, AND FIGHT AGAINST WILDFIRES

Ben Hubbard

LERNER PUBLICATIONS ◆ MINNEAPOLIS

For Roger and Noeline

Copyright © 2026 by Lerner Publishing Group, Inc.

All rights reserved. International copyright secured. No part of this book may be reproduced, stored in a retrieval system, or transmitted in any form or by any means—electronic, mechanical, photocopying, recording, or otherwise—without the prior written permission of Lerner Publishing Group, Inc., except for the inclusion of brief quotations in an acknowledged review.

Lerner Publications Company
An imprint of Lerner Publishing Group, Inc.
241 First Avenue North
Minneapolis, MN 55401 USA

For reading levels and more information, look up this title at www.lernerbooks.com.

Main body text set in ITC Garamond Std Book.
Typeface provided by Adobe Systems.

Editor: Nicole Berglund **Designer:** Lauren Cooper **Photo Editor:** Giliane Mansfeldt

Library of Congress Cataloging-in-Publication Data

Names: Hubbard, Ben, 1973– author
Title: Earth on fire : the science, history, and fight against wildfires / Ben Hubbard.
Description: Minneapolis : Lerner Publications, [2026] | Series: Gateway headlines | Includes bibliographical references and index. | Audience: Ages 9–14 | Audience: Grades 4–6 | Summary: "Wildfires have created damage throughout history, but now they occur more often and are more dangerous. Readers learn about wildfires, from their causes to how we can fight and prevent them"— Provided by publisher.
Identifiers: LCCN 2025013212 (print) | LCCN 2025013213 (ebook) | ISBN 9798765689554 library binding | ISBN 9798348028633 paperback | ISBN 9798765695302 epub
Subjects: LCSH: Wildfires—Juvenile literature | Wildfires—Prevention—Juvenile literature
Classification: LCC SD421.23 .H83 2026 (print) | LCC SD421.23 (ebook) | DDC 634.9/618—dc23/eng/20250725

LC record available at https://lccn.loc.gov/2025013212
LC ebook record available at https://lccn.loc.gov/2025013213

Manufactured in the United States of America
1-1013005-54823-8/22/2025

Table of Contents

Firefighters battle flames in California in January 2025.

Just days into one of the worst wildfires in California's history, the unthinkable happened—firefighters ran out of water. For hours, a team had battled the blaze tearing through Los Angeles's Pacific Palisades neighborhood. But around midnight, their hydrant ran dry. As the inferno engulfed buildings, firefighters could do little but stop and watch the flames.

"There's no water in the fire hydrants. The firefighters are there and there's nothing they can do—we've got neighborhoods burning, homes burning, and businesses burning. . . . It should never happen," Rick Caruso, the Palisades Village mall owner, told a TV station. The three massive water tanks that supply the Palisades were full before the fire started. So were all of greater Los Angeles's 114 water tanks. But there was simply not enough water to stop the multiple wildfires ravaging the city in January 2025.

A home in the Pacific Palisades burns during the January 2025 fires.

California had already been experiencing a months-long drought when the seasonal Santa Ana winds swept across the region in the New Year. The hot, dry winds struck Los Angeles with hurricane-strength gusts. Then, on January 7, fires sparked across several LA neighborhoods, including the Pacific Palisades, Eaton, Hurst, and Lidia. Soon fires were burning across the city with alarming intensity. Multiple buildings were quickly reduced to ashes. The devastation made headlines around the world. Within one week, thousands of homes and businesses had been destroyed, two hundred thousand people evacuated, and thousands of acres of land burned.

As often happens in emergencies, the fires brought out the best and worst in people. Many residents offered shelter to neighbors who had lost everything. Some brought clothing, food, and water to makeshift donation sites in parking lots. Others gave money to charities. But some people sought to profit from the disaster. They looted from deserted homes and set up scam charity and insurance websites. Arson was also suspected to be behind at least one of the fires. Whatever had caused the fires, it had taken less than a week to turn into one of the worst wildfire events in the state's history.

Volunteers assemble to help clean up after the January 2025 fires in Eaton.

Wildfires are not new in California, the United States, North America, or the world. However, wildfire season normally occurs in the summer months when temperatures soar and rainfall is scarce. California had experienced months of historically low rainfall before its 2025 fires. However, no one had expected them to strike in the middle of winter.

Some scientists say that this is the result of global warming, the buildup of greenhouses gases in the atmosphere caused by carbon emissions, brought about by climate change. They think that unless Earth's surface temperature can be lowered, every year will become the new worst wildfire season on record. Extreme wildfires fueled by climate change are becoming the new normal around the world.

Wildfires Through Time

Wildfires, also called forest fires and bushfires, are ferocious, unplanned fires. They can spread at speeds of 14 miles (23 km) per hour, reach temperatures of 1,472°F (800°C), and incinerate millions of acres of land. Thousands of people and animals worldwide die from wildfires every year. A wildfire can happen in almost any place at any time of year, but they often strike in summer, which is known as wildfire season.

Wildfires are not new. There have been large, destructive fires on Earth for almost as long as there have been plants to burn. In 2022 scientists discovered the planet's oldest wildfire. It took place around 430 million years ago in Wales, a country in the United Kingdom. This was a time before trees had evolved, so the oxygen level in the air was low and only a few plants thrived. How had this ancient wildfire happened?

"For fires . . . you really need three things: A source of fuel, which, surprisingly, we seem to have in sufficient amounts . . . you need a source of ignition, which is lightning strikes . . . and then you need at least 16 percent atmospheric oxygen," said Ian Glasspool, the scientist who made the discovery.

Wales, England, Scotland, and Northern Ireland make up the United Kingdom.

The ancient wildfire was surprising because there wasn't much oxygen or fuel on Earth at that time. Wildfires need oxygen, fuel, and heat to survive. But every wildfire starts with a single spark. The spark can be caused by lightning, a volcanic eruption, or even the sun's rays. However, most wildfires today are actually caused by people. According to the National Park Service, about 85 percent of wildfires in the United States are created by human activity. This activity includes leaving campfires unattended, throwing away lit cigarettes, and setting off fireworks carelessly. It also includes acts of arson, or deliberately lighting a fire to cause damage.

People should extinguish their campfires before they leave campsites.

Arson is a crime. But thousands of years ago, deliberately lighting a fire was a form of wildfire management. Native Americans, First Nation peoples, Native Hawaiians, and Aboriginal Australians were among the Indigenous peoples who lit small, controlled fires to aid ecosystems and to prevent bigger fires. This ensured there was less dry grass, branches, and fallen trees to fuel a large, uncontrollable wildfire.

An Aboriginal Australian man monitors a controlled fire.

However, during European colonization, these burns were prohibited. Fire was seen as too much of a risk to commercial logging businesses. People also wanted to protect their newly built wooden homes. During the 1800s, firefighting techniques improved and fire wardens were hired to put out wildfires in national parks. Fire was seen as a dangerous problem to be suppressed at all costs.

The result of these efforts was a buildup of dry material that contributed to big, destructive wildfires. One such fire occurred in the Midwest in 1871. It quickly became the worst wildfire in US history.

History's Worst Wildfire

In 1871 the American Midwest was having one of its hottest summers on record. In towns across Michigan, Minnesota, Wisconsin, and Illinois, there had been no rain for months. Many forests in the area had been cleared to make farms and the timber used to build homes. This was a time of great growth in the United States. But as the tree trunks, timber, and logging debris dried in the hot sun, it turned into the perfect tinder for a wildfire.

On October 8, fires sprang up in Michigan; Chicago, Illinois; and Peshtigo, Wisconsin. Fanned by the winds and fed by logging fuel, Peshtigo quickly became a firestorm. A firestorm is a wildfire so hot and strong that it creates its own wind system and is impossible to contain.

THE FIRE TRIANGLE

To start, survive, and spread, a wildfire needs a combination of heat, fuel, and oxygen. Today, we know this simple formula as the fire triangle. If one part of the triangle is removed, then the wildfire cannot survive.

- Heat is needed for a fire to ignite and keep burning. That is why wildfire season most commonly takes place during the summer.
- Fuel is needed to keep the fire going. Dry plants, trees, leaves, and wooden buildings all make good fuel.
- Oxygen is needed to support a fire. Wind feeds and fans a fire with oxygen at high speed.

Pine trees in California

Superheated flames ripped through the town of Peshtigo at tornado-like speed. Some people huddled in basements for shelter. Others rushed toward the river to escape. The fire had wiped out Peshtigo, eleven neighboring towns, and around 1.2 million acres (485,600 ha) of Wisconsin. Up to 2,500 people perished in the flames, making it America's deadliest wildfire.

But the wildfire did not end in Wisconsin. In Michigan, fires struck the towns of Holland, Port Huron, and Manistee. By midnight, the flames in Manistee became a firestorm that tossed hot cinders into the tops of large trees, setting them alight. As residents fled the town, reporter Bryon M. Cutcheon described the scene: "The steam fire engine burned in the street where it stood, the men and horses barely escaping with their lives."

The fires in Minnesota, Wisconsin, and Michigan were overshadowed by the fire that struck the city of Chicago. One of the best-known fires in American history, the Great Chicago Fire also began on October 8. The exact cause remains unknown. The Chicago fire raged for three days, destroying 17,500 buildings, killing over three hundred people, and causing millions of dollars in damages.

Today, the Great Fires of 1871 remain the deadliest in US history. But the factors that fed the flames—drought, wind, and dry fuel—are the same as those that make modern wildfires so deadly. What has changed is the frequency and ferocity of the wildfires that have struck

An illustration depicts residents of Chicago using a bridge to flee the flames during the Great Chicago Fire.

multiple countries over recent years. According to data from the University of Maryland, wildfires are becoming more widespread and burn twice as much land as they did two decades ago. Climate change, scientists say, is the major cause of this increased wildfire activity.

TYPES OF WILDFIRES

Surface fire, ground fire, and crown fire are the three main types of wildfires. Sometimes all three can occur at the same time.

- **A surface fire moves across the ground, burning leaves, branches, plant litter, and logging debris.**
- **A ground fire is a slow-moving fire that burns rotting wood and leaves on the ground. Ground fires are dangerous because they can smolder under a layer of snow all winter before reigniting in the spring.**
- **A crown fire burns in the crown, or top, of trees. Entire forests can burn down during a large crown fire when the wind changes direction suddenly. Crown fires are intense, dangerous wildfires that cause great destruction.**

A surface fire burns a field.

Wildfires Rising

The year 2017 was a game changer for wildfires. Portugal was hit by the worst wildfire year in its history. The country had been suffering an intense summer heat wave and months of drought. Then several wildfires suddenly started at once in Pedrógão Grande, in Portugal's Leiria district. Lightning may have been responsible for some of the fires, but arson was also suspected. The flames tore through eucalyptus and pine forests. More than one thousand firefighters were sent to battle the fires but

A firefighter battles flames in Abrantes, a town in Portugal, in 2017.

were unable to contain them. Meanwhile, walls of black smoke and red flames soared above trees in wooded areas. Some of the fires had begun at ground level but were now in the treetops. High winds pushed the fires from tree to tree, turning crown fires into firestorms.

On one rural road, forty-seven people died in their cars trying to escape the flames. Others perished while attempting to escape on foot. Several people avoided death by sheltering in water tanks. Maria do Céu Silva from the town of Nodeirinho hid her family in her home's water tank. This was a last resort. Silva had first tried to evacuate her mother by car. "My husband told me to put her in the van but she couldn't get in by herself so she told me: 'Let me die on the floor,'" Silva recalled. However, with the help of her son, Silva got her parents into the water tank. Around them, flames raged and winds tore roofs off houses. "It was like a horror movie," Silva said.

The Portuguese fires spread across the country and lasted for several months. In the end, 156 fires killed more than 120 people and burned about 1,235,530 acres (500,000 ha) of forest to the ground. Some people lost everything, and their anger smoldered long after the last flames had been put out. They said the government was to blame for not responding to the fires fast enough. Others said there was little firefighters could do when battling dozens of wildfires at the same time—especially firestorms. A firestorm fills the sky with wind and smoke and makes fighting fire from the air difficult, and sometimes impossible. As such, water-carrying aircraft often could not be used in the Portugal wildfires.

In large wildfires, aircraft are used to dump water on the flames. But the aircraft need visibility to fly. They also need water to collect to dump on the fires. But

A helicopter drops water on the 2017 Portugal fires.

today, climate change can lead to less water falling as rain in some areas. This means the ground is drier and lakes and reservoirs emptier.

Five years after the Portugal wildfires, a *Nature Geoscience* article showed that climate change had

ANATOMY OF A WILDFIRE

Every wildfire is made up of parts that influence how it burns and also how firefighters should fight it.

- **The point of origin is where the wildfire begins. It then spreads outward.**
- **Fingers are long, narrow, burning patches that stretch out from the fire's main section.**
- **The head is the fast-traveling part in front of the wildfire. It shows firefighters which direction the fire is moving.**
- **The heel is directly opposite the head. This is the part of the fire that spreads the slowest.**
- **A pocket is a small section of nonburning ground formed by fingers.**
- **The flanks are the side parts around the edge of a wildfire.**
- **Spot fires are often caused by burning embers carried by the wind and occur outside the main section of the fire.**

made the country the driest it had been in 1,200 years. This also meant its reservoirs were far below capacity. One reservoir in Pedrógão Grande was only 37 percent full in 2022. This was barely enough water to supply the local residents, let alone fight another wildfire. Without water in reservoirs, firefighters have nothing to spray on the flames and firefighting aircraft no water to collect.

The 2017 Portugal wildfires confirmed what climate scientists had been fearing. There had been a rapid rise in extreme wildfires around the world, brought on by global warming. The main cause of global warming is human activity, such as the burning of fossil fuels. Fossil fuels include coal that powers electricity stations, and gasoline in cars. Their use has led to an unsustainable rise in the temperature of Earth's surface. Drought and heat, the two main drivers of wildfires, are natural consequences of this rise in temperature.

A 2024 study in the journal *Nature Ecology & Evolution* analyzed satellite images of wildfires. The study showed that the number of extreme wildfires in the world had doubled in the last twenty years. The scientists also found that the majority of recorded extreme wildfires worldwide had occurred since 2017, the year of the Portugal fires. The scientists warned that the rise in these extreme fires was creating an alarming feedback loop. Large carbon emissions were being released by wildfires. This carbon caused more global warming, which, in turn, caused more wildfires.

Smoke in the Air

After the Portugal wildfires, many countries thought about summer differently. Weeks of hot, dry weather without rain were no longer desirable. Instead, they began to make people nervous. In 2018 and 2019, there were serious wildfires on every continent except Antarctica. Fires broke out in places not usually affected by wildfires, such as the United Kingdom, the Canary Islands, and New Zealand.

Indonesia was soon to suffer its own massive wildfire. In 2019 Marlizar, a volunteer firefighter, was working in the country's Riau Province. He noticed smoke rising from a section of peatland. The peatland was on fire, and the flames quickly grew. Peat is a type of dense, wet soil made from decayed plant matter. It is rich in carbon and highly flammable. People use slabs of dried peat as firewood.

Marlizar tried to beat back the flames with a tree branch as his colleagues rushed for help. Within an hour, the fire had swept across 12 acres (5 ha) of land. When Marlizar's colleagues returned with a hose two hours later, the whole region was on fire. A rescue operation now had to take place.

The fire spread fast and sparked many more fires. These wildfires blanketed Indonesia and its neighboring countries in a thick, smoky haze. Burning peatland had made the fires highly toxic. The 2019 Indonesian wildfires burned through millions of acres of peatland. This released hundreds of millions of tons of carbon

A firefighter in 2019 in the Riau Province

into the atmosphere. The haze hung over the region for weeks and caused serious breathing problems for nine hundred thousand people.

The losses of land, property, and people are only some of the consequences of wildfires. Another is air pollution. The Indonesian fires showed that wildfire smoke not only adds to greenhouse gases already in the atmosphere, but it can also have a devastating effect on people's health.

Smoke hangs over a burned forest after the 2019 Indonesian fires were extinguished.

The 2019 Indonesian fires were not the only large wildfire emitting a vast cloud of smoke that year. Australia was also rocked by one of its worst wildfires. The wildfires were known as the Black Summer Bushfires. Scientists calculated that these fires let more smoke into the atmosphere than ever seen before anywhere in the world. The particles from the smoke stayed in the atmosphere for over eighteen months. Thousands of Australians were affected by smoke inhalation. According to the *Medical Journal of Australia*, the wildfire smoke caused over three thousand hospitalizations and 417 deaths.

WHAT'S IN WILDFIRE SMOKE?

Wildfire smoke is a mix of toxic gases and tiny particles such as ash. The tiny particles are harmful to human health because people can breathe them deeply into their lungs. The particles can cause irritation and damage and spread to other parts of the body. These particles can stay in the air for weeks, unlike the other gases in wildfire smoke. These gases include the harmful carbon monoxide, sulfur dioxide, and nitrogen dioxide.

Considering the severity of the Australian fires, this was no great surprise. Following months of drought and the hottest temperatures on record, fires swept through the country's southeastern bush and forest. Lightning was to blame for many of the fires. The wildfires kept burning for months and destroyed about 60 million acres (24.3 million ha) of land. Over three thousand buildings were destroyed and thirty-three people killed in the flames. But there was something else that also grabbed headlines—lost wildlife.

It is estimated that about three billion animals died in the Black Summer Bushfires, including about sixty thousand koalas. Koalas, one of Australia's most recognizable creatures, became an endangered species due to the fires. The number of animals killed is staggering, but many more creatures were also made homeless by the fires. These creatures included 143 million mammals, 2.46 billion reptiles, 180 million birds, and fifty-one million frogs.

Yet only six months after the Australian wildfires ended, the forests were showing signs of recovery. After two years, many burned eucalyptus forests were found to be regrowing. To help, the Australian government invested AU$200 million to support the recovery of local wildlife. The World Wildlife Fund came up with a plan called Koalas Forever to double the number of animals in the country.

Australia was not the only country with new wildlife

Fire burns amid a thick haze in the Australian state of New South Wales in 2019.

initiatives. Following its own 2019 wildfires, Indonesia partnered with the United Nations to enact a plan to stop extreme wildfires. The plan brought together government agencies and local communities. Their first aim was to prevent small fires from growing and combining to become larger fires. The second aim was to educate local people about the risks of throwing away cigarette butts, leaving cooking fires unattended, and burning land to create room for palm oil plantations. Palm oil is a profitable crop used in candy and cosmetics. The Australian and Indonesian plans showed that people are not helpless and action against wildfires is possible.

Fighting the Flames

In 2023 an extreme wildfire broke out in a surprising place: Maui, Hawaii. Maui's residents were prepared for national disasters such as hurricanes and volcanoes, but the wildfire on August 8 caught them by surprise. The island had been experiencing heat, drought, and winds strong enough to bring down power lines.

One of these downed power lines set off a spark that lit the dry vegetation around it. At around seven o'clock in the morning, residents of Lahaina, a town in Maui County, reported seeing smoke around the town's outskirts. By two o'clock, the Maui Fire Department reported that this fire was out. However, the winds were so strong that the fire's embers flared up again. Then the nightmare for Lahaina started.

The Waiola Church in Lahaina, Maui, burns down in 2023.

By four o'clock that afternoon, flames were tearing through the town and burning homes and businesses to the ground. Residents tried to flee by car but were soon trapped in traffic. Some people abandoned their cars and fled to the shore to huddle in the water. Others were burned alive in their cars. By the morning, all that was left of Lahaina was a smoldering ruin. Authorities said that wind gusts of 80 miles (128 km) per hour had caused the fire to travel at 1 mile (1.6 km) per minute. With 102 people dead, the wildfire became the fifth-deadliest fire in US history.

Thousands of Maui residents lost their homes, businesses, and family members. They demanded answers from local authorities. Many said they were not given evacuation orders and emergency sirens stayed silent. They were distressed to learn that fire hydrants had run dry, stopping firefighters from dousing the flames. This was partly due to water pipes melting in the fire and leaking water. This both used up the town's supply of water and weakened its flow to other places. Maui's water pressure was also dependent on electric power, which was affected by the number of downed power lines, to pump water to the hydrants. These downed power lines also meant getting to the fire was difficult. But without water, firefighters were forced to focus on evacuating people, not fighting the fire.

Some experts said that having water was irrelevant. The out-of-control wildfire was simply impossible to battle, they said. "When it comes to wildfire, especially wind-driven, weather-driven fires, the Fire Department is not going to be able to stop the fire. It's really about what we can do to make our homes safer," said Maui Fire Chief Brad Ventura.

With extreme fires becoming more and more commonplace, firefighting has never been more difficult. But firefighters are finding new ways to tackle extreme wildfires and educate the public about preventing them. Traditionally, engine crews make up the front line of a firefighting attack. The crews use fire engines and hoses to attach to fire hydrants and douse the flames. But for large forest fires, a number of specialists are involved. These include wildland firefighters, who clear away brush, logs, and other fuel. Wildland firefighters dig long ditches in the ground. These starve an approaching fire of fuel and create a line it cannot cross.

The best wildland firefighters can become elite firefighters known as hotshot crews. These experts travel to a wildfire's head to predict where it will go. They then use chain saws, explosives, and digging equipment to cut off the fire's fuel supply. One of the most dangerous firefighting jobs is carried out by smoke jumpers. Smoke jumpers are daredevil firefighters who parachute from

A smoke jumper exits a plane during a training session.

planes into the middle of a wildfire and dig firebreaks to stop it from spreading. This is important work in areas that fire engines cannot access. In these situations, firefighters also depend on help from the air.

Water-dumping airplanes, or water bombers, can drop thousands of gallons of water on a fire in one attempt. They can also spray a fire retardant over areas in the fire's path that have not yet burned. Helitack crews do the same job from helicopters, where they can hover and land firefighters in awkward areas.

A water bomber extinguishes a wildfire.

THE WORLD ON FIRE

At any given time, there is a wildfire happening somewhere on Earth. Many of these fires are dangerous and destructive—but not all of them. Fires also took place before there were humans to start them.

As part of the natural world, wildfires can have benefits. Fires can clear away dry and decaying underbrush and allow new growth to begin. This can give rise to new life. However, many of today's wildfires do not follow a natural pattern because they are caused by climate change. Scientists say that longer fire seasons in North America are linked to changes in spring rains and snowmelt, which have been lessened by climate change. Finding a way to combat climate change, therefore, is an essential step in fighting wildfires.

Controlled burns clear away brush and other flammable materials to prevent wildfires.

Aerial firefighting is highly dangerous. Planes have to fly only 100 to 200 feet (30 to 60 m) above fires to dump their loads, and accidents can occur. In the United States, thirty-seven aerial firefighters have died in the last decade. Aerial firefighting, however, has become increasingly important with extreme modern fires. In 2023 Canada experienced its worst wildfire season on record. Starting in May, wildfires burned through 37 million acres (15 million ha) of forest and released billions of tons of carbon into the atmosphere. Smoke from the fires spread all the way to the United States and Europe. High winds and dry conditions meant many of the Canadian blazes became crown fires and firestorms. In the province of British Columbia, aerial firefighters normally plan to fly around 560 water bomber missions a year. In 2023 they flew 816.

In 2024 the world experienced one of the hottest summers on record and many wildfires occurred. In response, one specialized water bomber was put into high production. The Canadair is a firefighting plane that can hold 1,621 gallons (6,136 L) of water, fill up from lakes, reservoirs, and seas within twelve seconds, and fly as low as 100 feet (30 m) to douse flames.

As long as smoke doesn't make aerial bombardment impossible, water bombers are the key to fighting modern wildfires. As the 2025 wildfires in Los Angeles grew, Canada was quick to send some of its water bombers to help fight the flames.

Wildfires Today and Tomorrow

In February 2025, the LA wildfires were finally put out. Residents could return to what remained of their homes, businesses could contemplate reopening, and the cost of the fires could be calculated. The fires had burned over 50,000 acres (20,234 ha) of land, destroyed over twelve thousand homes and businesses, and left at least twenty-seven dead. The total cost to rebuild in LA would be around $250 billion, according to experts. This made it more expensive than the 2018 Camp Fire, California's deadliest wildfire.

The remains of a neighborhood in the Pacific Palisades after the 2025 fires

The Camp Fire also made headlines for its terrible impact. It burned through 153,336 acres (62,050 ha) of Butte County, destroyed over eighteen thousand structures, and caused eighty-five fatalities. The total cost of the fire was more than $12 billion. However, the fire was also a lesson in preventing unnecessary wildfire deaths.

The fire had been caused by a faulty power line, which set fire to surrounding dry vegetation. The fire quickly spread. Residents of the town of Paradise described a hailstorm of hot embers raining down

Winds carry the Camp Fire across hills of California in 2018.

on their homes. Many people tried to flee by car but were caught in gridlock. Some became stuck behind abandoned cars or fallen power lines. In Paradise's streets, people were burned alive in their cars. Others perished after exiting their vehicles and running. Some people were able to wait the fires out in their homes, while others died doing the same thing. Eventually, heavy equipment bulldozed cars and power lines off the town's exit roads. Buses then evacuated people from the burning town.

After a trial, the local power company was found guilty for the fire. Its power lines had not been properly serviced. But some of the town's planning was also at fault. In 2005 a state fire document said Paradise was at risk of a serious wildfire. As predicted, in 2008 a wildfire did indeed strike. Afterward, a Butte County grand jury said Paradise needed to create wider exit roads. Otherwise, people trying to escape a future wildfire could be caught in traffic. After the 2008 wildfire, Paradise residents began their wildfire planning. They practiced drills and had their bags ready.

However, the size of the town's exit roads remained the same. People died in the 2018 fires as a result. Paradise's emergency management director Jim Broshears said the town had been ready—just not for a wildfire of that size. "We didn't have a plan that addressed a fire that would be everywhere. . . . We had an evacuation plan built for a wildland fire. We had a hydrogen bomb. . . . We were so overmatched," Broshears said.

Cars are stuck in heavy traffic.

Is it possible to prepare for extreme wildfires such as the 2018 Camp Fire or the 2025 LA Wildfires? There are certainly lessons that can be learned from each one to help plan for the future. All communities at risk need to have evacuation warnings and sirens that everyone can hear. People must also have access to escape routes or fireproof shelters to hide from the flames.

Cities need readily available water tanks and generators that can get water to fire hydrants, even if electrical power goes down. Future building needs to take place away from forested areas, and construction materials need to be fire-repellent, wherever possible. Those people in wildfire risk areas can also consult local fire guidelines for protecting their homes. This often involves making sure there is no flammable fuel such as dead trees near houses and buildings.

Fuel on the ground is repeatedly blamed for feeding some of the worst wildfires of the last twenty years. This is the period when scientists say wildfires have become more extreme. It is in part due to the policy of fire suppression. In North America, Hawaii, and Australia, Indigenous peoples knew the importance of small wildfires to burn dry fuel and prevent a larger wildfire

A man sets a controlled fire in Zambia, a country in Africa.

from developing. However, European colonization in the 1800s prohibited controlled burns and fought to put out all fires immediately. In many ways, the consequences of this policy have helped lead to the extreme wildfires of today.

Fuel, however, is only one part of a wildfire. Drought, heat, and wind-charged oxygen to carry the flames make up the other parts. These are related to weather conditions made worse by climate change. Until humans commit to reducing global warming, extreme wildfires will keep happening. But we can help prevent wildfires by staying safe with fire, such as campfires or fireworks, before they can grow. And when wildfires do strike, we can help those in need.

Important Dates

430 million BCE	A large wildfire takes place in what is now Wales, a country in the United Kingdom. It is the first known wildfire in the world.
1871	The worst wildfires in US history sweep through the Midwestern states of Minnesota, Wisconsin, Illinois, and Michigan and lead to the Great Chicago Fire.
2009	In response to a 2008 wildfire in Paradise, California, a Butte County grand jury says Paradise needs to create wider exit roads for mass evacuations.
2017	A wildfire in the Pedrógão Grande region of central Portugal becomes the deadliest in the country's history, killing 120 people and burning 1,235,530 acres (500,000 ha) of forest.
2018	The Camp Fire in California devastates 153,336 acres (62,050 ha) of Butte County, destroying over eighteen thousand structures and causing eighty-five fatalities, becoming the deadliest fire in the state's history.

2019 A wildfire in Indonesia releases millions of tons of carbon dioxide into the atmosphere and covers many neighboring countries in a thick, smoky haze.

2019–2020 The Australian Black Summer wildfires kill about three billion animals, including sixty thousand koalas.

2023 A wildfire razes Lahaina, Maui, to the ground.

Canada's worst wildfire season on record sends clouds of toxic smoke to the United States and Europe.

2024 A study shows extreme wildfires have increased by more than ten times over the last twenty years, creating a feedback loop of carbon emissions.

2025 Los Angeles is struck by one of the worst wildfires on record. Several prominent neighborhoods are destroyed, and at least twenty-seven people are killed as a result.

Source Notes

7 Matt Hamilton and David Zahniser, "Fire Hydrants Ran Dry as Pacific Palisades Burned. L.A. City Officials Blame 'Tremendous Demand,'" *Los Angeles Times*, January 8, 2025, https://www.latimes.com/california/story/2025-01-08/lack-of-water-from-hydrants-in-palisades-fire-is-hampering-firefighters-caruso-says.

11 Jonathan Amos, "Earliest Evidence of Wildfire Found in Wales," *BBC*, June 27, 2022, https://www.bbc.com/news/science-environment-61929966.

16 Marisa Fancy, "The Great Fire of 1871," Northern Michigan History, accessed July 15, 2025, https://northernmichiganhistory.com/the-great-fire-of-1871/#google_vignette.

20 "Portugal Forest Fire: 12 Survive by Hiding in a Water Tank," *BBC*, June 19, 2017, https://www.bbc.com/news/world-europe-40324006.

31 Greg Allen, "A Downed Power Line Is Officially Blamed for Last Year's Maui Wildfire," *NPR*, October 3, 2024, https://www.npr.org/2024/10/03/nx-s1-5137353/maui-lahaina-hawaii-wildfire-report.

38 Paige St. John et al., "Must Reads: Here's How Paradise Ignored Warnings and Became a Deathtrap," *Los Angeles Times*, December 30, 2018, https://www.latimes.com/local/california/la-me-camp-fire-deathtrap-20181230-story.html.

Selected Bibliography

Aratani, Lauren, Maanvi Singh, and Abené Clayton. "LA Residents Receive Short Reprieve from Santa Ana Winds Fanning Deadly Flames." *Guardian* (US edition), January 16, 2025. https://www.theguardian.com/us-news/2025/jan/15/california-wildfires-warnings-los-angeles.

Baker, Mike, Kellen Browning, and Nicholas Bogel-Burroughs. "As Inferno Grew, Lahaina's Water System Collapsed." *New York Times*, August 13, 2022. https://www.nytimes.com/2023/08/13/us/lahaina-water-failure.html.

Demony, Catarina, and Miguel Pereira. "Five Years on from Wildfire Tragedy, Portugal Again at Mercy of Heat and Drought." Reuters, July 20, 2022. https://www.reuters.com/world/europe/five-years-wildfire-tragedy-portugal-again-mercy-heat-drought-2022-07-20/.

Estep, Kim. "The Peshtigo Fire." *Green Bay Press-Gazette*, reprinted by the National Weather Service, accessed July 15, 2025. https://www.weather.gov/grb/peshtigofire.

"Indigenous Fire Practices Shape Our Land." National Park Service, March 18, 2024. https://www.nps.gov/subjects/fire/indigenous-fire-practices-shape-our-land.htm.

McCarthy, Mia. "Newsom: LA Wildfires Could Be the Worst Natural Disaster in US History." *Politico*, January 1, 2025. https://www.politico.com/news/2025/01/12/newsom-wildfires-worst-natural-disaster-california-00197715.

Swannell, Cate. "Bushfire Smoke Responsible for over 400 Excess Deaths." *Medical Journal of Australia*, March 23, 2020. https://www.mja.com.au/journal/2020/bushfire-smoke-responsible-over-400-excess-deaths.

Learn More

Britannica Kids: Wildfire
https://kids.britannica.com/students/article/wildfire/629045

Havemeyer, Janie. *Wildfire Survival Stories*. Child's World, 2024.

NASA: The Science of Wildfires
https://www.jpl.nasa.gov/edu/resources/teachable-moment/the-science-of-wildfires/

National Geographic Education: Wildfires
https://education.nationalgeographic.org/resource/wildfires/

Spilsbury, Louise. *The Science Behind Raging Wildfires*. Cheriton Children's Books, 2022.

Starr, Abbe L. *Climate Change Solutions*. Lerner Publications, 2023.

Index

Photo Acknowledgments

Image credit: Jon Putman/Anadolu/Getty Images, p. 6; Tayfun Coskun/Anadolu/Getty Images, p. 8; Sarah Reingewirtz/MediaNews Group/Los Angeles Daily News/Getty Images, p. 9; WLDavies/Getty Images, p. 11; Karl Weatherly/Getty Images, p. 12; Penny Tweedie/Getty Images, p. 13; Bloomberg Creative/Getty Images, p. 15; Wikimedia Commons PD, p. 17; ElenVD/Getty Images, p. 18; PATRICIA DE MELO MOREIRA/AFP/Getty Images, p. 19; PATRICIA DE MELO MOREIRA/AFP/Getty Images, p. 21; Wahyudi/AFP/Getty Images, p. 25; Anton Raharjo/Anadolu Agency/Getty Images, p. 26; SEAN DAVEY/AFP/Getty Images, p. 28; AP Photo/Matthew Thayer/The Maui News, p. 30; Darin Oswald/Idaho Statesman/Tribune News Service/Getty Images, p. 32; AFP PHOTO/JAIME REINA/Getty Images, p. 33; Eric Thayer/Bloomberg/Getty Images, p. 34; Brian van der Brug/Los Angeles Times/Getty Images, p. 36; Karl Mondon/Digital First Media/The Mercury News/Getty Images, p. 37; Allkindza/Getty Images, p. 39; Gideon Mendel/Getty Images, p. 40.

Cover: AegeanBlue/Getty Images.